Plan Your Novel in as Little as One Day

How to Be a NaNoWriMo Winner
by EM Lynley

NaNoWriMo or National Novel Writing Month is an annual event for writers around the world. It offers participants an opportunity to write a 50,000-word novel with the support of others. It may be just the motivation you need to get writing.

- Have you been dreaming of writing a novel for years and didn't know how to tackle the daunting task? This book is for you.
- Have you attempted NaNo and found your story and inspiration flagging long before you hit 50,000 words? This book is for you.
- Are you an experienced writer or published author who wants a comprehensive planning tool to enable you to plot, write and revise more quickly? This book is for you.

This method will enable you to build the foundation for a complex novel, with engaging characters and an emotional journey that will keep your readers turning pages. Accompanying worksheets and full instructions make the process almost foolproof.

All the Tools to Write a Complete Novel in 30 Days
HOW TO BE A NANOWRIMO WINNER
A Step-by-Step Plan for Success
EM LYNLEY

How to Be a NaNoWriMo Winner

By EM Lynley

Other Books by EM Lynley

Novels
Jaded (forthcoming November 2013)
An Intoxicating Crush
Lighting the Way Home
Hostile Takeover
Italian Ice
Rarer Than Rubies
Sex, Lies & Wedding Bells

Novellas
Gingerbread Palace (forthcoming December 2013)
Venus Envy
A Lesser Evil
Brand New Flavor
A Christmas Bonus

Non-Fiction
Tax Tips for Authors
How to Revise Your NaNoWriMo Novel (forthcoming December 2013)

Editor
Bedknobs & Beanstalks
Going for Gold Olympic Anthology
Wicked Good
Rumpled Silk Sheets

How to Be a NaNoWriMo Winner

By EM Lynley

First Edition, October 2013

First edition
ISBNs
Print: 978-0615900872
E-book: 978-1301815708

Published in the United States by
Silk Road Press
San Francisco, CA

Contents

Introduction

I've been writing fiction for most of my life, but I didn't start giving it serious time until I spent a year and a half on medical leave. I had unlimited amounts of free time and a lot of ideas, so I started writing.

My first long piece was what I now realize is called a serial. I wrote a chapter a week and posted it for my friends to read. Soon hundreds of others flocked to my website and I was hooked. That first serial story turned into a novel-length piece, but it wasn't quite a novel. Not because of the length, but because it really didn't have the structure of a novel: a beginning, middle, and end.

I kept writing and eventually took the plunge and sent something to a publisher. First a short story that was accepted and then a novel, which was also accepted. It sold quite well and the publisher begged me for another one.

Now I was in serious trouble. I didn't really know how to write a novel. I knew how to write a story, with not much clue where it was going and how long it would take to get there. I worked on several projects for the next year, never knowing how long each piece would be, and I was pretty much always surprised.

Then a writer friend of mine, Gina X. Grant put me on to Holly Lisle's writing clinics. Finally I understood how to collect the pieces of a story and arrange them so that writing became fun, and not a matter of crossing my fingers each time I sat at the keyboard.

I started using Holly's worksheets to build a story, and it clarified a lot of elements I had just been guessing about previously. For a couple of years I used her method exclusively. Then in 2012 I came across John Truby's book *The Anatomy of Story* at the San Francisco Public Library.

I was hooked. He expanded on many of the elements I already used in planning my stories from Holly Lisle, but as a screenwriter and studio consultant, he used some screenwriting techniques that I found even more helpful.

The end result is that I've combined elements from Truby and Lisle along with some of my own methodology based on dozens of writing books I've read, courses I've taken and trial and error. I've constructed my own set of story planning worksheets. I've designed a new version just for this book, and most of the book will discuss how to fill in the sheets and how to fine-tune your planning process.

The bottom line is that with a thorough story planning process I can now develop the plan for a novel in about a day or two. With the basic skeleton of the story in place, I have been able to successfully write—and sell to publishers—a novel in a month. I've done this four times in the past year alone. Each of these novels clocks in at over 75,000 words, so you can be sure the process can lead you to rich, layered characters and a complex story.

And I'm thrilled to share my process with you.

I wish you as much luck and success as I have found.

Before you get started, please download the Worksheets you'll need for Chapters 2 and 4 from my website at **http://www.emlynley.com/Nano**

Chapter 1: Planning Your NaNo Novel

Whether this is your first year at NaNoWriMo or your tenth, it takes exactly the same amount of work to get be a winner—hitting the magic 50,000-word mark by November 30.

How difficult or easy that task will be depends in a large part on how you approach the challenge. If you have to dig a hole, you'd rather use a shovel than a spoon, right? If you need a really big hole, then you'd love to get your hands on one of those big excavating machines.

If you want to run a marathon, you don't show up at the starting line wearing flip-flops. You may make it the whole 26.2 miles, but you'll be in agony most of the way.

Writing a NaNo book is no different.

Give yourself the right tools and the process will be a lot easier, and absolutely more fun.

Why Plan?

Over the years I've discovered the hard way that planning a story is the difference between a smooth writing experience and one where I'm pulling my hair, digging into a tub of Ben & Jerry's, or deciding to watch re-runs of *Law & Order* instead of staring at a blank page. Even worse, the pressure of needing to get a certain word count each day made it all even worse.

"I'm never going to finish this," I used to tell myself,

and if you say that enough, you *will* start to believe it.

But the key to winning NaNoWriMo (hitting 50,000 words) is having something to write every single time you sit down at the computer, or notebook. It's not just the security of having an idea where the whole story is heading, but when you're not writing, you will find yourself thinking ahead to the next section you'll be writing, synthesizing what you've just written, and figuring out scenes and plot points you never dreamed of before.

Far from cramping your writing style, planning—*not* outlining—actually can free your brain up to be more creative. You've already made some of the big decisions in the story, so your creativity can focus on the details.

I know a lot of you are ready to write off the rest of this book, or skip directly to the tips and tricks. My suggestion is for you to at least work through the planning tools in the next chapter about character building, and fill in some of the worksheets. Once you see how powerful even a little planning can be, you'll find the task of writing that much easier and more fun.

The NaNo rules only say you can't start writing the story until November 1, but there's nothing to stop you from planning the story earlier. In fact, if you wait until November 1 to start thinking about the story, you are almost guaranteed to fail.

Why?

Because a good story has layered characters and plot. Some of these layers come from a familiarity with the characters. It's not a matter of knowing what high school she went to or whether he wears boxers or briefs. It's about knowing what the characters are going to do in particular situations, how they speak, and how they interact with other characters. Most of all, it's about what inner forces drive them, and how those forces will affect them throughout the course of the book as the plot unfolds.

Like many writers, I get to know the characters better as I write. By the end of the manuscript, I know a lot more than at the beginning, and usually I have to go back and rewrite a scene or change early dialog because the character wasn't fully formed in my brain.

A little planning can minimize how much of that extra work is required. And the more you know the characters, the better you can mess with them by knowing what events will result in the most conflict and tension, which is what makes a great story.

Look at the film *Vertigo* as an example. Most people can manage to overcome even a fear of heights to save a person on a roof or ledge, which happens in a scene late in the film. However, James Stewart's character has more than a fear of heights. He failed to save someone in the past, so he's got a huge emotional challenge, as well as the psychological one. You can build in this kind of huge emotional impact on your characters—and readers—when you know what makes the characters tick at their deepest levels.

There are as many plot-related reasons to start planning in advance. If you happen to be working with a complicated story with subplots or a mystery, you will have a lot of details and threads to keep track of. You will also need to work hard to make sure everything fits together and makes sense.

Starting that process in October means you will already know where you're going to hit the snag and come up with a solution before the NaNo clock starts ticking.

I was writing a book dealing with smugglers. I had sketched out the key plot events and sequence, but I was stuck trying to figure out how the contraband items got from point A to point B. I put the story on hold for over a month while I bounced ideas off friends and tried to make them work with the rest of the story.

You want to minimize or avoid the chance of unexpected plot problems during November. In fact, if you're a new writer, I don't suggest a mystery/suspense plot unless you have lots of time to figure out how connect the dots.

But we're getting off track.

You can see how planning your NaNo book in advance is only going to increase the chances of:

- Finishing the book
- Having a more intricate, layered story
- Deeper, multi-dimensional characters
- A first draft that won't need as much revision
- A less stressful NaNo experience

For the Pantsers

Are you one of those die-hard pantsers who think planning interferes with the story and stifles creativity? I used to be you.

My first few novels and stories started out with a flash of inspiration and I just kept typing away, without a clue where the twists and turns would end up. It was fun. It was exciting when the story flowed. But on the days when I was tired or stressed, my whimsical muse was nowhere to be found.

Those were the days when I did stare at the blank page and then grab the TV remote. I lost a lot of days of writing when I didn't feel motivated or excited.

This is one form of writer's block. The I-don't-have-anything-to-write version. And it sucks. Big time. For a professional writer like me, it also means nothing accomplished and another day closer to a looming deadline.

The antidote is planning. It may be as simple as working through some character-building exercises or making a list of cool scenes that first come to mind (more on that later, in Chapter 3).

This lets you save up some inspiration for the days when you just don't know what happens next in the story.

Whether you decide to plan or not, I do have some strategies for getting back on the keyboard when you really can't think of another thing to write, but you're still not finished with the story. You know it happens. And I'm here to help when it does.

Plan vs. Outline

A Plan is not an Outline

I'll bet when you saw the word "plan" in the blurb you made a face like you'd sucked on a lemon. Am I right?

Who out there got flashbacks of outlining in a course or the recalled dreaded Roman numeral format. I never could remember if it was numbers then letters, or letters then numbers.

Well, I'd raise my hand too if I had to outline something ever again. Then I'd run screaming from the room.

I'm not talking about an outline at all.

Not only do I not like outlines, I think it's boring to outline the typical novel.

Notice the word "typical."

You may need more structure if you write a mystery because the sequence of events and details is a key element in the story. There is more than one order to place events and clues and revelations, but you need to get them all in there.

It still doesn't mean you need an official outline.

So how is a plan different?

A plan is just that, an idea of what's going to happen, or what you would like to happen, and how you're going to make it happen.

I took SCUBA diving lessons years ago when I was living in Japan. One of the first things you learn: "Plan the dive, then dive the plan."

Writing is exactly the same way. It doesn't always end up where you think it will, but you can prevent some stress and headaches with a little forethought.

If sequence is important to your story, like mystery or thriller, it lets you play around with the best order for events.

With my Story Planning Worksheet, you'll be answering some of the really big picture questions like what does your character want and why, and who is going to stop him. Once you decide on a character arc, the steps will practically write themselves.

That's the goal of planning: get the big overarching issues decided, and you can have fun with the details. You will have more time for the details and you will have a more enjoyable experience letting go of the little things.

It's like baking a wedding cake. You have a deadline for the project. If you have the basics done early, like baking the cake base and mixing all your colored frostings, you have a lot more time for making leaves and flowers and adding in those little silver balls. What are those things called anyway?

In the next chapter we're going to work on assembling the ingredients for the cake.

Chapter 2: Story Planning in 11 Steps

Download the Story Planning Worksheets from my website at **http://www.emlynley.com/Nano**

How to Use the Story Planning Worksheets

I've designed a special worksheet to follow each of the eleven steps. I recommend you download and print out the PDFs. It will make your planning much simpler and you'll have a record of everything you've established, which you can refer to while you are writing.

Before we go further, I will say that this book is not intended to be a comprehensive guide to every aspect of writing a novel. I'm not going to bog you down with discussions of structures and acts and writing theory.

That's all good stuff, and personally I love to read it and try to apply it to my own writing, but it's not going to get your NaNo novel written. And that's my goal.

We'll focus on a step-by-step technique—not a formula—to build the foundation on which you can write a 50,000-word novel in a month.

Step 1: Premise

Premise is a concept that comes from screenwriting. In Hollywood, studios and producers want the whole story summed up in a single sentence. Everyone is Hollywood busy, and apparently they don't have time for a whole paragraph, much less a page about the story.

The advantage of developing a premise sentence is that it forces the writer to get to the point, to boil the story down to its pure essence. That's the premise.

It probably sounds like a tall order, since you haven't worked on your characters, plot, or anything at this point. How can you possibly come up with a winning premise first? And that's a great question. You don't have to. You can skip to the storyline development, then go back and find your premise.

If you take a look at the Worksheets, you will see I've got room for several evolving versions of your premise. As you complete a step, you'll reevaluate the premise until it's strong enough to build your novel.

However, according to screenwriting consultants, and particular John Truby, author of *The Anatomy of Story*, this is where most stories break down. The premise isn't robust enough to hang an entire film—or book—on. That's why we'll come back to the premise several times before we even start thinking about the plot specifics. Baby steps.

What if I don't know what I want to write about?

Hang in there, I've got exercises for you too.

So we'll start with a draft premise, do some more planning, then come back and fine tune the premise line after we've made a lot more decisions about the story. You may find yourself looking at the story from an entirely different perspective after this process, and that's fine. Because that's the point of the planning sequence. It works, and I have used it many times. Each time I find the process more fun and get more creative.

I'll use last year's NaNo novel as an example of how planning produced a much stronger story than I had originally expected to write.

In 2012 I was planning a novel about a winemaker who runs a family winery that comes under attack from a big corporation wanting to buy him out and he's forced to sell to get out of financial trouble. Since I write romance—gay romance—the love interest had to be someone who would immediately be in opposition to the besieged winemaker: a financial analyst from the conglomerate. The story was going to focus on how the winemaker changes his mind about selling after the analyst gives him financial advice to get his business out of debt. The analyst risks his job—valuing the winery--so he could help the winemaker (now his lover) fight off the takeover. To me it felt like it was absolutely the winemaker's story. He's upset about losing the winery, and with help from the finance guy, he not only saves the business, but finds love.

That's what I thought, until I started my process.

My draft premise was

Winery owner saves his business with the help and love of a financial analyst.

Sure, that might sound a bit boring, but the final product is a lot better, and you'll see why later.

If you have an idea what your story will be about, write down your premise on the first line of the Story Planning Worksheet (SPW).

Don't have any idea yet?

No problem. While everyone else is writing their premise, grab about 5 sheets of blank paper. or use the back of something from the recycling bin at work or school.

• On Sheet #1, make a list of the kind of people that you find interesting.

College professor, an escaped convict, a rabbit breeder, a hairdresser, a homeless woman. Write down at least ten examples.

You may already have some idea of who you want to write about, but keep listing others just to get your brain working outside your usual comfort zone. We might use those other folks later.

• On Sheet #2, write down a list of interesting circumstances or problems. They don't need to be connected to the first list. Just get down on paper the kind of problems that interest you.

Losing a job, running for president, hitting a dog with your car, starring in a play on Broadway, graduating from college, meeting your favorite celebrity, losing your wallet.

To get a problem big enough for a novel, the problem your main character faces must be one that will turn his world upside if he can't solve it. Now that you've jotted down a few ideas, go back and blow them up larger than life, so they're big enough to ruin your character's life.

Go back and write at least ten disaster scenarios.

Here are some examples: a plane crashing, the president getting kidnapped, a sick child dying, getting wrongfully convicted of a crime.

• On Sheet #3, write down topics that interest you or would like to write about.

It could be related to you and your life or job, or it could be completely different. Just make a list of people, places, things, situations, problems, even a scene you've thought about or a dream you had.

Now you've got a lot of possibilities, and you've got your brain warmed up. Go back through the third list and circle all the people. They are possible characters.

• Take a fourth sheet of paper and draw a line down the middle so you have two columns.

On the left side, write down the people you circled from Sheet #3. Then go back to the first sheet, and circle all the people who sound interesting, then write those on Sheet #4.

Now do this for all the situations and problems. Write them down in the right column of Sheet #4.

Now match up people and problems. Draw lines, circles, whatever you want.

• On Sheet #5 write down a sentence about each person-problem combination.

Example 1

Pablo is a student from Peru studying in Los Angeles, and his visa is about to expire. That's a big problem.

Miranda, a struggling actress loses her wallet with a winning PowerBall ticket in it.

Let's have Pablo find Miranda's wallet... and what could that lead to? He could use the credit cards, or sell them, or he could visit her. Is he a stalker or a fan? Let's say he goes to visit her and she invites him in. What kind of story could you see between these two?

If he's really a struggling writer: she might help his career.

Or maybe he's engaged to a Korean student named Jae, but they're going to be separated. Again, the actress might be able to help. Now the story is less about the actress and it's turning into one about the student.

Nothing there seems really earth shattering. While these people might have interesting problems, I'm not sure I can hang a whole book on Pablo and Miranda.

Let me dig into my own list of interesting people and scenarios.

Example 2

I'm a fan of spy thrillers, so I'm going to try my hand at one here. It's got a little Cold-War vibe to it, but it's got a lot of potential for conflict and very big stakes, which is what we want.

Brant, a CIA analyst, has just gotten a warning from his boss that he's in trouble for letting some classified information go missing.

David, another analyst, wants Brant's job, and actually took the information so Brant would get blamed.

Draft Premise

I can already start forming a premise with these two characters, and I'll be expanding it as I go along with the rest of the worksheet.

Brant's a CIA analyst and he must protect his job from David, who will try anything to get Brant fired.

That sounds like a good start.

You can connect an infinite number of people, problems, circumstances, so play around until you think you've at least found two people you'd like to write about and a problem or situation for each one.

We'll flesh them out as we go along.

You can spend as much or as little time on this brainstorming exercise as you need until you hit on a promising combination of main characters and challenges.

Step 2: Evaluate the Premise

Decide whether your premise is enough to carry an entire book.

(If you haven't got a full premise yet, don't worry, skip down to step 3)

- Is there enough story here? Is your main character's problem big enough to change his entire life if he doesn't solve it?
- Is there enough change along the way to show a transformation in one or more characters?

Example 1

Take our Peruvian student. He's about to be separated from his fiancée due to the visa problem. We've gone past the wallet story, and hit on a life-altering situation for him.

That's not a bad start, but I don't think I can expand it into enough to fill a whole book. If I do, it's probably going to stretch the story past its natural limits.

When you first start writing, it's often difficult to tell how long the finished piece will be. I still can't judge the precise length of my books, but I know the minimum length will depend on how much plot there is and what side stories I include.

I aim for at least two main plotlines. With romance, you *always* need two: the romance plot and an external problem plot, which in the case of my 2012 NaNo book is whether the guy will lose his winery. I added a couple of other smaller plots, but let's not get ahead of ourselves. Try to find another plot line out of your premise.

Write down at least five plots or story lines related to the draft premise or to the characters you've chosen.

Let's look at some examples.

The Three Musketeers: you've either read the book or seen one of the films.

The premise would be along the lines of "Young man goes to Paris to join the Musketeers and proves himself when he's caught in political intrigue."

The main plot is the political one, with Cardinal Richelieu's attempt to embarrass the queen and the Musketeers and D'Artagnan save her and are rewarded.

But there's more going on. There's D'Artagnan's love interest, Constance, who also connects the Musketeers to the political storyline, and a third plot concerns the animus between Milady and D'Artagnan.

It's an ambitious book, and I'm not suggesting yours be as complicated, but you get the point. There are a lot of other plots you can hang from your draft premise here.

Let's have another look at Brant and David in my spy story.

What other storylines can I bring in?

David tries to throw suspicion on Brant that he's actually a Russian spy.

Brant really *is* a Russian spy.

Brant has become loyal to the US and has been passing poor information back to Russia so he won't harm US interests.

Brant is supposed to debrief a Russian defector, Vassily, who is actually defecting in order to become a double agent.

Vassily knows Brant from Russia. In fact, he's been sent to keep an eye on Brant.

Brant has an American girlfriend, Carla, who would be disappointed to discover Brant has been lying about everything to her.

That's more than five, and many of them are intertwining. I think draft premise is enough to turn into a novel, when I bring in aspects of Brant really being a spy.

Next, we'll work on developing the main characters into people with enough layers to support a novel.

Step 3: Needs and Wants

These are the elements which will make your premise, or proto-premise stronger, and may change how you approach the story.

Many writing books call these needs and wants "motivations" or "goals." They look at goals, motivation, and obstacles. Sometimes it's called the GMC model: goal, motivation, conflict.

We're going to take a slightly different approach that will add another layer—or more—to the characters and their goals.

There are two "motivation" lines.

Each character should have both surface desire and a hidden need.

Surface Desire

The surface desire, also called the desire line, is what the character wants in the story. The traditional GMC model uses this approach.

The actor wants a part, or the actress who lost her wallet wants a friend who isn't trying to use her. The guy running for president wants to be president.

Those are easy to list. If you haven't already got it as part of your premise, write down what your main character wants in your novel. It has to be pretty big, since it's the key action he is going to pursue during the story. It will drive all his actions.

In my winemaker novel, the winemaker wants to save

his family winery.

Simple and to the point. Nothing hidden there.

Example

In my CIA spy story, Brant wants to avoid being discovered as a spy so he can stay in the US.

His rival, David, wants Brant's job.

Vassily wants to get Brant to provide good information for Russia, and he also wants a nice comfortable American life.

Write down what your main characters want on your Worksheet. List a few goals/desires if you want.

Now for the fun stuff. We're going to give everyone even more motivations.

Hidden Need

What your character really needs in the story is a function of his traits.

On the surface, the character has a very obvious goal. But underneath, an unfulfilled need is driving him. He may not even know what this empty part of him wants, but it is going to affect nearly everything he does.

To get the hidden need, you must give your characters a weakness. Perfect characters will be boring. Readers do not identify or care about perfect characters. Look at Stephanie Plum in Janet Evanovich's series about a bounty hunter. Stephanie is far from perfect. She's always making mistakes and getting into trouble. It's what keeps us turning pages.

Now it's time to develop your main character's traits,

a set of strengths and weaknesses which will define them and everything they do during the story. In fact, these traits will also suggest how they will react to every plot point and to each other.

Choosing Character Traits

In Chapter 3, I have a list of character traits for you to use as a jumping off point if you find it difficult to decide on the appropriate traits for your characters.

Pick three strengths that make sense for who the character is:

Example

Brant, CIA analyst:

- Intelligent, thinks fast on his feet
- Personable, and is good at reading people (except for David)
- Loyal to the US (he is now, and that will be important for many reasons)

Carla, Brant's girlfriend

I'm not sure how she is going to fit in yet, but let's see who she might be. We can always adjust these later once we've selected more elements of the story.

- Honest
- Trusting
- Connected in Washington. Niece of a general or someone high up in the intelligence community.

Add in a "Superpower"

One key to interesting characters is to give them an unlikely combination of traits, and make sure to give each character his own "superpower" or "cause."

What's a superpower? Flying? Seeing through steel? Nope, unless you're writing a superhero story.

A superpower is your character's unique skill or passion. It should define him and set him apart from 99.9% of other people who have the rest of his characteristics and traits. When someone mentions the topic, the reader should immediately think: "Bob's an expert in that!"

Take Robert Langdon in *The Da Vinci Code*. He's an expert in symbology. It's natural he'd be called when a man dies with a lot of symbolism at the death scene. Indiana Jones is the only available expert on Tanis, so the G-men come looking for him when they can't find Abner Ravenwood.

What could I choose for Brant's superpower? He's a former Russian spy, so maybe he has the most extensive knowledge of Russian language and practices of some obscure sector of the Russian government. This expertise is precisely why he's selected to debrief Vassily.

The superpower can set the events of the story in motion.

Sometimes that's called the inciting event. For many stories, there is too much of a coincidence that our hero would be around when some big disaster or problem occurs. So make it less of a coincidence, because he's the most likely person to be there. And make sure his special knowledge also allows him to solve the key problem in the story or avoid the disaster.

Carla's superpower can be her connection to some very important people because they are her relatives. She's likely to hear what's going on in the intelligence community, and even if her job isn't related, it makes sense for her to be involved, without making her an analyst too.

Choose a Weakness for Your Character

I've you've been watching television or films during the past decade, you've probably noticed how popular it is to have heroes with flaws. Take Batman. He's got a lot of dark secrets and they drive him just as much as his strengths and his surface desire to fight crime.

In many recent dramas, the anti-hero is the new protagonist. This is a character who has perhaps more flaws than strengths.

There are two levels for each weakness. I told you we were going to add layers, and this is how we do it. But if you're following along on the worksheet, you'll be in good shape. It will all become clear, I promise.

This distinction and expansion of the character's weakness is from John Truby, and it really adds a lot to the mix of character development.

Level 1: Psychological Weakness:

At this level, the weakness affects only your character. He suffers from his weakness, and as long as he can stand the consequences, he is unlikely to find the need to change.

Level 2: Moral Weakness:

This level of weakness affects others, particularly ones the hero cares about. He may discover a reason to change when he understands how he is hurting someone else.

Take a few minutes and skip to Chapter 3 and read the section Why Weaknesses Matter More Than Strengths. Then come back here and to the SPW.

There's a good chance you've changed your mind about your character's weakness after reading. The choice of weakness is the absolute key element for building your character and his arc.

Pick a weakness for each character.

You can go back to the Traits list and exaggerate nearly every strength to get a weakness.

Curious becomes nosy

Loving becomes obsessed

Intelligent becomes too good for most of the people around him.

Example

Brant's weakness is dishonesty. He lies for a living, literally. He came to the US as a Russian spy, and had to lie to fit in. Now he wants to stay, so he has to lie to Russia about the value of the crappy intelligence reports he sends them.

Worse, he's lying to Carla.

There are several reasons why the weakness is

extremely important.

The weakness sets up the conflict.

Because Brant is hiding his true identity, he is susceptible to Vassily's threats to tell the Russians *and* the Americans. The lies put everything Brant values at risk

The weakness drives the character arc over the course of the book.

The main character must be forced to confront his weakness and through the events of the book, he will overcome the weakness, as he experiences his revelation or reversal.

I don't suggest you use one of the strengths you've already chosen for your character as the basis for his weakness. You may end up changing your choices again after we get to the next exercise.

Write the weakness in the Worksheet

Example
Brant's weakness: dishonesty
Carla's weakness: excessive loyalty/patriotism

Brant's weakness: dishonesty

Psychological effect: It's tough to live your life when you are lying every day. But Brant knows he has to keep lying or he'll get in trouble or have to go back to Russia

Moral effect: Brant has set himself up for disaster with Carla, and with every other aspect of his life unless he keeps lying. But he needs to keep lying, which is going to put him at odds with Carla and her suspicions.

Hidden need associated with weakness: Brant really wants acceptance, to be himself and to be valued for his true personality. He can't get any of this, or really trust anyone else, until he can be honest.

Carla's weakness: excessive patriotism/loyalty, instilled in her from childhood by her family

Psychological effect: She's not quick to trust anyone, though she does almost automatically trust anyone her family trusts.

Moral effect: She makes it difficult for others to be honest about feelings or opinions when they don't agree with her.

Hidden need associated with weakness: Carla needs to trust people before she can relax with them. Her real need is to feel safe and comfortable.

By understanding these levels of strengths, weaknesses, and underlying needs you know what's wrong with your characters and how they are going to have to change.

Now look how many more layers Brant and Carla have after that last exercise. He's distant from people when he's hiding something, which is going to strain his relationships more, and the result is people want to trust him *less*, so he's losing what he wants to preserve.

The great thing about going through these steps is that you know a lot about your character and how he thinks, reacts, etc. These strengths and weaknesses will drive the action once we get to developing the plot. But you notice I haven't discussed names, birthplace, favorite food, or the age Brant lost his virginity? Why not? Because those elements don't drive the deeper aspects of the story that make up your premise.

If you are writing a story where one of these things

had a profound effect on how the character acquired his traits, then you will want to give some careful thought to these aspects as well and make the part of the evolving character profile.

The premise doesn't rely on descriptions or even a character's back story. How you write the story *built* on the premise will be affected by those decisions. Back story may explain how he acquired his traits, and that's what it's there for.

I know why Brant doesn't tell the truth, and I can see how it's going to lead to disaster, forcing a seismic shift in his world that makes him transform into an honest guy.

You can also get a feeling for how the traits will affect the plot. I don't know what's going to happen in my story, but I can see how Brant and Carla are likely to respond to a given situation, based on their traits. This will come in handy later when you are writing and you don't have a clue what happens next. You can toss out a "what if" at a character and you know how it's going to go down.

Step 4: Character Arc

If you had any doubt about which character is your main character, you won't after this section. If you're writing romance, with two equally important main characters, you may want to focus more on one character's journey than the other. In fact, you don't need an arc for both characters. If this is your first novel, I suggest you stick with one character arc. Better to do one extremely well than to run out of time or space to resolve the other main character's arc.

If you cannot decide who should be your focal character, choose which arc is going to be bigger and more emotional and you'll have your answer.

Example 1: With NaNo story last year, about the winemaker, his arc involved him learning to trust someone to care about his winery as much as he did. My financial guy's arc had him giving up a job in a career he loved, for the hero. It's clear which arc was more emotional and transformational. All along I thought it would be the winemaker's story, but as I worked through these steps, the other character's arc became so clear, and he took over the story. Had I focused on the winemaker, it would have been boring. Yes, he changes and I put him through plenty of hell, but he didn't come out a drastically different person as a result.

We know Brant's weakness before we start writing, so we know who Brant is going to be at the end of the story: a guy who is honest.

Your main character's weakness will be resolved

through the events of the story.

What kind of things could happen to Brant in the story?

What would be the worst thing that his dishonesty would cause? His boss could find out and he'd be in jail. Carla could find out, then he'd upset her and end up in jail because she turned him in. That's even worse than if the CIA boss finds out first.

I've just discovered the climax of the story by throwing the *worst* thing at my main character, or at least the worst thing I can think of right now.

I still don't know how we're going to get there, but I have a goal to work toward when I'm planning and later when I'm writing. Knowing that key point doesn't lock you in as much as the pure pantsers are thinking right now. Because you may just figure out something even worse once you start writing, or later in the planning process. We've really just touched the surface.

The key to engaging a reader's emotions is by forcing the characters to their breaking points and having them make the most difficult decisions and become better people. Every test, every source of conflict and tension will be connected to the strengths and weakness you select for your characters.

Deep weaknesses will lead to profound transformations, leaving your readers wondering how on earth the hero can recover from each blow. If your character's main weakness is shyness, and the big test is that he has to talk to a girl he's got a crush on, it's not deep enough. Make his big test the need to give a speech to a room of one hundred executives to land a big project, and his career—or the fate of funding for a hospital in Guatemala—rests on him overcoming the fear, then you've got high stakes, which lead to high emotional connection.

I used this key formula in Chapter 3
Beginning characteristics x Plot = Ending characteristics

For Brant
Dishonest, fed-up spy x Plot = Honest guy who has the support of Carla

I don't know yet what plot events will happen, but I do want Carla to accept him and support him by the end of the book. I want Brant's honesty to be rewarded, and maybe I'll even figure out how he can stay in the US without going to jail.

Let's recap our progress so far in the spy story example. We started with a couple of random pieces of information: Brant is a CIA analyst who's really a Russian spy. He's under threat from the co-worker who wants his job and the Russian defector who can turn him in to both sides.

We know Brant's strengths and weaknesses, and we know a bit about the other characters. I also know what Brant's character arc will be, how he will change and how at least one other key character fits into Brant's transformation.

If you still don't know where your story and characters are going, that's. And it's okay, because you can write down ten different ideas in ten minutes and think about each of them for a minute or two each to weed some out right away.

For me, it takes longer to explain the process than it does to go through all the steps.

But the one thing we haven't discussed yet is another essential piece to a great story.

Step 5: The Villain/Opponent

The villain is just as important as your main character. He is the reason the main character is doing whatever he is trying to do (the surface desire). Our hero is trying to get something first, or get something back from the villain. The villain is there to keep him from achieving his desire, and he can do that by manipulating the hero's weakness.

You see how this is all connected? I hope some light bulbs are going off.

The process has a lot of moving parts and at first it may sound a bit daunting, but if you take it step by step, you will build up a great story, because you've laid a foundation that can support all the fun scenes that you'll write during NaNo month.

Back to the villain.

Who is going to keep Brant from staying in the US?

We have a lot of candidates: Vassily, David, Brant's boss, Brant's Russian handlers.

How to choose?

Who has the power to cause the most trouble for Brant? Vassily can turn him in to the US or to Russia, or both. He makes the most powerful opponent.

So now we know who the opponent is. What's his story?

There are a few crucial elements to the perfect opponent:

- He should be equal in strength to the main character, but he should appear stronger at first.

- He knows or senses the hero's weakness and uses it against him.
- He must have a valid reason for wanting to stop the hero from achieving his desire. At least it's valid to the villain, and it should be to your reader, even if they don't want the opponent to beat the hero.
- He should have good traits as well as bad ones. An all-bad opponent is as boring as an all-good hero.
- Develop him as well as you develop the hero. Go through the same process with strengths, weaknesses, desire, needs (psychological and moral).
- Your hero and opponent should overlap on some issues, goals, or desires. Put them into direct conflict.
- The opponent's weakness can be exploited by the hero, which is how the hero gets the upper hand.
- Your hero must beat the opponent through *his own actions*. If his house is in foreclosure and the opponent is the bank manager who won't give him another month before kicking the hero out, the hero cannot win the PowerBall and pay off the mortgage. He must *earn* his desire through his internal transformation, as he overcomes his weakness.

With all of that in mind, go to the Story Planning Worksheet and fill in the traits for your villain.

Example

Vassily:
Desire: Stay in the US
Need: protect himself, at any cost

Strength: smart

Strength: experienced in espionage, more than Brant or David

Weakness: love of money and material comfort, dishonesty

Psychological: he lies about everything, and he has no moral code, and he also doesn't know whom to trust.

Moral: his lies mean no one trusts him completely, so everyone uses him for their own means.

If you haven't discovered your villain yet, go back to your hero's desire line, traits and weakness. Make a list of five to ten potential opponents based on those weaknesses and goals. Think through a new premise using each one of the potential opponents. Write them all down if it helps you choose which one is going to put your hero through his paces, make his life miserable, and force the hero to confront his weakness and eventually win his desire and fulfill his hidden need.

Then, flesh out your opponent with his own set of strengths and weaknesses. As you continue this process, additional elements of the story will naturally occur to you. Write those down too.

Now go back to your latest premise at the top of the worksheet. As you develop more pieces of the puzzle, the premise will evolve. Write each new version down so you can see how you're able to fine-tune the premise into a powerful and workable idea.

Step 6: Character Web

If you think I'm talking about Spidey, sorry to disappoint.

The character web is a way to envision how all the characters interact with each other.

This is one of my favorite parts of the planning process. It allows me to cement the interrelationships between characters that will drive the conflict. Having a solid character web will give you almost unlimited options for ideas while you're writing.

You have the hero, the second main character, and a main opponent or villain. You'll also need a variety of supporting characters.

Allies

These are people the hero can trust, rely on, get assistance or comfort from. That's pretty straightforward. Your main character needs some friends, co-workers, or even the elevator operator, who's on his side. Often these allies are the ones who get him going on the right path, or have his back in danger.

Make a list of five possible allies, their connection to the hero or his desire, and how they might help him.

Other Opponents

These characters are trying to keep the hero from one or more of his goals/desires. Again, this concept isn't hard to fathom. Who else wants what he wants? Who wants to make sure he doesn't get it? Why?

Make a list of five possible opponents (besides the villain), their connection to the hero or his desire, and how they might hinder him. If they are connected to the villain or to the hero's weakness/challenge, even better.

False Allies

Here's where we start having some fun. Take a look at your allies. Which of them might be hiding a secret? Which of them is not really on the hero's side, but wants the goal, or is passing information on to an opponent?

Look at every ally to see how he might really be an opponent. You'll only need one, but look at each one and decide how he can betray the hero. Choose the one that would hurt the hero the most to discover the treachery. Think Iago in *Othello*. Othello believes Iago is helping him, while in fact he's undermining Othello all along, through Desdemona, who represents Othello's weakness--jealousy.

In one of my books, I have a character who is an actor. Some personal photos are sent to the tabloids with a devastating effect on his career. He has several obvious opponents in the story, but it turns out his best friend did it, thinking it would help him. She had good intentions, but the main character felt a terrible betrayal.

False Opponents

These are a little more subtle. You don't necessarily need for one of the baddies to secretly be the hero's ally, though it's one way to do it. Another is if someone the hero never suspects is an ally comes to his assistance.

Analyze each opponent for ways he might eventually help the hero, and why. The most surprising one is going to get the biggest reaction from your readers.

However, one thing to be careful about here is telegraphing. While you want the shift in this character's loyalties to be surprising, watch that you don't make him too negative to start. Readers will spot that early on and you'll lose the emotion the character should generate when he reveals himself.

A great example is Snape in the Harry Potter books. For most of the books he's one of Harry's worst enemies, but then we find out he's been looking out for Harry in his own way. When that is revealed, it's quite a shock. It happens so far into the series, and that's why it works so well.

Try these other ideas:

The fake opponent is never the center of the action, but is on the periphery, so readers don't really notice him. (Agatha Christie uses that method, and so do other mystery writers).

The fake opponent doesn't have to be particularly evil, but he should do something extraordinary when he does help the hero.

For more on the character web, including how to diagram the relationships, please read "Character Web" in Chapter 3.

Step 7: Reaching for the Desire

You know what your hero wants, and who stands in his way. You also know both characters' strengths and weaknesses. Now list the ways the hero could try to achieve his desire. Whether he succeeds or not doesn't matter yet. What is his main plan? How does the opponent keep him from the goal? How do the allies and other opponents fit in?

You don't need a lot of detail as you consider ideas here. Just jot down random thoughts in this section of the Worksheet.

Example 1

Let me use some from my 2012 NaNo story. Austin (the winemaker) wants to keep his winery from getting bought out by his boyfriend (Simon)'s boss. Simon is stuck in the middle and sometimes that puts him at odds with Austin, and at others he's at odds with his boss.

Simon knows his boss wants to buy Austin's winery, but refuses to give him information or work on the project.

Austin borrows money from the bank to cover short-term financial problems.

Simon's boss gets information from the bank manager.

Austin asks Simon for suggestions in how to make the winery more profitable.

Simon's boss retrieves data about Austin's finances from Simon's computer.

Simon's boss buys the loan from the bank and threatens foreclosure if it's not repaid.

Austin blames Simon for the data leak and the threat

by the boss.

Austin dumps Simon because he cannot trust him or his loyalties.

Simon finally has to choose between his job and Austin

Austin is forced to sell some land to cover the loan.

Simon finds a buyer for the land who will resell it to Austin later.

Example 2

Let's see what could happen in Brant's story.

Brant's living a comfortable life in the US, sending back useless data to Russia. He likes living here and feels no loyalty to Russia.

Vassily shows up as a defector, and Brant recognizes him and the threat he represents.

Vassily is only pretending to defect, to position himself as a spy to help Russia

Brant has to prove that Vassily isn't really defecting, in order to prove his own loyalty to the US

Brant eventually has to tell Carla, because if she believes him, her powerful family connections could save him.

How do his opponents affect these plans?

David plants false information or purposely misinterpreting real data to implicate Brant; he doesn't know that Brant really was a Russian spy.

David drops hints to Carla, who gets suspicious and starts digging into Brant's past or following him around. Maybe both. Eventually David's suspicions and what Carla sees makes her think David is right. She will have to confront

Brant at some point.

Vassily threatens to tell the truth to the US and to the Russians, who think Brant has been sending real intel.

Vassily and David work together, though David doesn't know Brant is really a spy or why Vassily is helping.

Vassily tries to arrange Brant's murder to save himself.

Brant finds himself evading Carla and lying to her about other things, and she becomes even more suspicious.

Carla tells one of her relatives her worries, further pressuring Brant.

Write your own ideas down on the Story Planning Worksheet.

These ideas will become a backbone for the plotting, and should comprise the middle section of your story, all of which we'll get to later.

As the book progresses, the hero should be more and more desperate to get his goal, and resorting to more extreme actions.

Suppose your character wants money and his plan is to rob a bank. How would your particular character go about planning the bank robbery? You've set him up with traits, weaknesses, inner needs, and a group of friends, enemies, and random others. Now how will all of these influence his plan?

Step 8: Battle/Climax

How does the opponent try to stop the hero? What is the pivotal moment or action where they come face to face?

This can also be where the worst thing possible happens to the hero—preferably at the hands of the opponent.

Example 1

In my 2012 NaNo story, the battle comes when Simon the financial guy has to choose between his job and Austin, the winemaker. Simon has tried to help Austin and to hold off his boss's attempts to get information about Austin's finances that would help the boss force Austin to sell. Finally, the boss has what he needs—he bought out Austin's loan from the bank.

Now while Simon is choosing the job he lovers or the man he loves, Austin is also facing a huge decision. Austin doesn't trust Simon and he doesn't like asking for help. His father shows up offering to cover the loan, but Austin doesn't take the money. Here, Austin's battle is not only with Simon over his role in the buyout, but with his father.

Both characters have to make big decisions.

Simon's weakness: he wants success and money and somewhat self-absorbed in trying to reach his goal. You can see how the boss can manipulate him by offering him the job he wants (a carrot) and threatening to fire him if he doesn't cooperate (a stick)

Simon's pivotal moment when his boss asks him a final time for information he can use to get Austin's winery. Who will he choose, and why?

Austin's weakness: He won't trust anyone and he thinks he needs to do everything himself to be a success. He's too proud to accept help when his father offers it. You see how Simon's boss can pressure Austin financially, knowing he won't get any assistance.

Austin's pivotal moment comes when he has to choose between his own dream of taking the winery in a new direction or saving the winery by selling the land that will allow him to realize his dream for the future. Simon offers a solution, but can Austin trust him, or admit to needing help?

Example 2

Brant is trying to fend off Vassily, David and Carla. He's juggling Vassily and the Russians, forcing him to offer some important document, and David could catch him when he accesses it.

Carla's already suspicious and following him around, when she sees Brant meet Vassily and another Russian guy. She sees him give the document and confronts him about it later, with her own threat to turn him in.

Now he has to tell her the truth because he can't lie at this point. He has to hope that everything he has come to love about the US is true and that if he shows his loyalty he might not get the worst punishment. He chooses between keeping his dream—he could just kill Carla—and losing it, because he does the right thing. He can turn in Vassily, expose his treachery to the Americans, and hopes Carla will back him up.

But the only way Brant can hope to win is to tell the truth. It allows him to get out from under Vassily's threats and possibly get Carla's help.

On your Worksheet, write down several ideas for the pivotal moment for each main character. It will involve the villain or opponent and the character's weakness. You should come up with several different pivotal moments, perhaps piling on other opponents or other weaknesses, so the hero has a lot to deal with at once, and choosing one option precludes any other choice.

He has to have lost everything, or be about to lose everything, or give up everything he thinks he wants and needs, in order to achieve his desire.

Now we've set the story up for how the character will overcome his weakness.

Step 9: Self-Revelation

Your hero should be in a position where he's forced to make a terrible choice: either he overcomes his weakness or he loses his goal/desire. He looks inside and realizes he's been wrong all along and he can change.

Of course you can't have a sudden 180-degree shift in the character. That's not realistic and your reader will cry foul. It has to be believable, and it will be when the choice is life-or-death, or as close as you can get in your story. You must also have shown his resistance to make this change earlier, so that the idea for the shift is already in his mind, and in the reader's mind as a possibility. Show him finally realizing something he's been resisting.

By demonstrating sufficient motivation—averting disaster or saving the universe—you can make the self-revelation work.

A downside of the self-revelation is that readers are very probably expecting this to happen. You can add a twist to it so it doesn't occur in the way they expect. During this planning process, you may not yet have enough information about the events of the story to decide on how to make the self-revelation more surprising, but as you write, and get to know the characters, you will definitely get a feel for what each of them will do, and how it will all lead to this point.

Example 1

A classic example is Rick in Casablanca. He's made the deal for Ilsa to stay in return for granting the exit visa to Laszlo. He's used Ilsa's love for Laszlo against her, knowing she'll make the sacrifice to get her husband to safety. Then he realizes that she'd be miserable with Rick, and anyone who loves enough to make the sacrifice deserves to be with her true love. Rick knows the right thing is to let Ilsa go with Laszlo, and in the end he gives up what he wants the most, and becomes a better person for it.

Example 2

Brant stops lying. He needs for Carla to believe he never did anything really wrong. He cares too much about her opinion of him, even if telling the truth will put him in danger, or jail. He has to trust she will do the right thing in turn and refute David's false allegations and help him turn Vassily in too.

I just have to make sure I have Brant thinking about telling the truth, weighing consequences, and finally deciding it's the only alternative, and that his situation will be even worse if he does not. He must consider what he'll lose and what he'll gain.

Double Reversal

In this variation of the self-revelation, the villain (or other main character) also undergoes a character shift to overcome his weakness/challenge and becomes a better person because he and the hero learn from each other.

This doesn't work for every genre, but if you're writing romance, you'll want to include some element of the double reversal where both partners realize they have been sabotaging their relationship and/or the other conflict in the story, and creating more problems for each other.

Example

Brant's story doesn't lend itself to Vassily having a

double reversal, because he is too unlikable a character to deserve one. With a more sympathetic opponent it might work. David doesn't qualify for one either, because his rationale behind framing Brant is self-centered, not out of patriotism, like Carla.

Carla may undergo her own self-revelation in recognizing her weakness made it difficult for Brant to come clean earlier, or he might have told her the truth, and defused his own dangerous position before Vassily showed up and ignited the situation.

Step 10: The Ending

When I first started writing, I never had much clue where the story would end up. I also didn't care. I liked writing and just kept going until it felt like a good place to end the story.

I suspect a lot of writers do the same thing.

What that meant was in the middle I often didn't know what should happen next, and I sat staring into space racking my brain for ideas.

Then I read a lot of writing books and took some writing classes, and I understood how important it is to have some clue where you're heading, and where you want the story and characters to end up. When you do that, you have a spot to write toward, rather than just meandering aimlessly until it feels like an ending.

This also helps work through the middle, which is where most writers start to give up, especially in NaNo. You get all excited the first week, maybe even ten days in, tapping away, and then you're stuck. If you know where you want to go, you're more likely to arrive.

Some people liken the process to driving across country. I start in California and start driving. If I don't know where I want to end up, I might not even be going in the right direction. I can take any road, then turn onto another if the name of the town sounds fun, or I like the highway number.

How many of you do that when you're on vacation and have a week until you get back to work? Probably no one. You have your limited vacation time and you want to get something out of it.

NaNoWriMo is a lot like that.

You have 30 days to finish your book. The goal is 50,000 words, but we all would like to have a finished novel at the end, not just 50,000 words.

So, like your vacation time, your NaNo time is precious. Make sure you get where you want to go, by driving in *that* direction. You may take some unexpected side trips, but you won't get completely off track.

How do you know where you want to go?

Remember we have set up our hero to have a goal—his desire—and a plan to achieve it. We also gave him some strengths and weaknesses. The weaknesses are holding him back from the goal. In order to achieve his goal, he will have to overcome the weaknesses and become a different person, which we discussed in the self-revelation.

And that brings us very close to the end of the story, but not quite.

The true ending is often called the "new equilibrium."

Your hero has his goal—or he's changed so much he decided on a different goal, and he's satisfied. That's his new equilibrium. He has defeated the opponents, overcome his personal challenges, and dealt with all the conflicts we threw at him during the story.

So who is your hero at the end of the book?

Go back to your list of beginning character traits, strengths and weaknesses. He should still have the strengths, but he's overcome at least one weakness.

Write down his new strengths on the Worksheet.

Does he still have a weakness? It's not realistic for someone to change completely, so you may want to keep one of the less vital weaknesses, one that wasn't a key factor in his internal character arc.

If your hero was selfish, amoral and charming to start, he's not too likely to become Mr. Perfect, unless the only way to get his desire was to become moral and start thinking of others.

Example

Brant keeps his job and Carla, and he is safe from the clutches of the Russians. Maybe Brant even gets some little award for turning in Vassily and a couple of other guys they didn't know about. Brant uses his knowledge and expertise to discover other potential spies.

Now Brant's dishonesty has turned into honesty. He feels better about himself and his future, and he knows he won't have any more problems with Carla over his need to lie. He doesn't need to lie to get what he wants—or thinks he wants—or what he really needs.

Does he still have a weakness? Probably. I haven't decided what it is yet. I have plenty of time, since I won't need to figure it out until I get closer to the end.

There are certainly many aspects of the story I haven't even touched on yet, but I have all of the most important elements—the foundation—in place.

The Other Method

If you read the section in Chapter 3 “Why Weaknesses Matter More Than Strengths,” you’ll remember my little formula

Starting character x Plot = Ending character

It’s perfectly fine to have an idea who your hero will be at the end, even if you haven’t worked through the steps on his character arc.

You can simply define your ending character’s traits, then work backwards to create a path for him to get there.

If you want your hero to be kind to animals, brave and intelligent, then figure out who he needs to be at the beginning. It’s a bit tough to make him smarter, so we need to concentrate on the other traits to develop appropriate beginning weaknesses.

He can be timid, maybe even afraid of animals, or he might own a cattle ranch and meets a person who thinks he doesn’t take good care of his horses and cattle, and he changes through their influence.

There are many ways to work this transformation. Now that you’re almost done with the big picture elements of your NaNo novel, you may decide you’re not completely happy with some aspects of the character arc.

It’s fine to go back and tweak. In fact it’s the main reason we’re doing these exercises before we even start writing a word on the story. If one element of the character or plot isn't working, the time to discover that is before you're 10,000 words and a week into November.

Step 11: Revisiting the Premise

Now go back over all your answers as you developed your characters, traits, goals, conflicts, opponents, arcs, etc., and your latest version of the premise.

How does your premise sound now?

Can you rewrite one or two master sentences to sum up your character's key problem, goal, weakness, need, conflict and change?

Example:

Brant, a CIA analyst, is in fact a Russian sleeper spy who's happier in the US. When a new defector threatens to reveal his secret, Brant has to choose between his new American values and the threat of jail—or worse.

Write your final version of the premise on the Story Planning Worksheet, and then you're ready to start working on the story skeleton.

If your premise isn't yet ready for prime time, go back to the steps that you aren't happy with, and work through them again.

Then write your new premise at the top of the Worksheet.

Write it on a Post-It and stick on your monitor.

Cross-stitch in on a pillow.

Now let's get to the plot.

If you haven't read through the more detailed discussions of character development, read Chapter 3. Otherwise, skip to Chapter 4, Constructing the Story Skeleton

Chapter 3: Developing Your Characters

Introduction to Character

For me, the most important part of the planning process is developing the characters. There are two reasons for this:

Characters sell, plain and simple. Readers keep buying Sue Grafton's alphabet series because they love Kinsey Milhone. We're currently up to the letter W, and honestly, the mysteries have not been particularly compelling for about the last decade, but Kinsey keeps drawing me and millions of other readers again and again.

We don't care what she does, we just want to hang out with her for another few hundred pages.

Sookie Stackhouse? How many of you read the books that became the True Blood series? Enough for HBO to build a series on them.

It's the same for films and television. Why do we keep watching James Bond films? Because we love Bond, not the stuff he does. We want to see him win.

Readers will follow characters they love (or hate) past the border of logical behavior, if the characters are compelling. That means you can get away with a lot more if readers love your characters.

Reason 2: It took me a long time to figure out the reality of Reason 1. By nature, I'm a plot-centric writer. I think of all the events that will happen in my stories, then I figure out how to push the characters through the fascinating series of hoops I planned so meticulously.

And to be honest, my first few novels got some reviews where readers said that's how the story felt. They didn't get an organic connection between the characters and the plot, and the characters were a little underbaked.

I admit my mistake. So I went on a quest to create better characters. I have a lot of books about writing characters, from psychological approaches to dialog. I didn't get much out of most of them, until I hit upon the key piece of information:

Character and Plot are connected. You can't have one without the other, and if you start with character, you will be building plot at the same time.

Why Weaknesses Matter More than Strengths

In an earlier section I discussed the concept of starting out with a character with issues and how the plot action affects the character, creating the character arc.

Character x Plot = Ending

Let's rewrite that a little bit

Starting Character x Plot =
Ending Character

This section explores how to create both the weaknesses and the relevant plot points to bring the character to a new set of values, behaviors and attitudes. It draws on John Truby's techniques in The Anatomy of Story.

You want your characters to change over the course of the story. To do that, they must have problems that get solved through the plot, so they emerge better people at the end.

But more than problems, characters must have weaknesses. These weaknesses define them, their actions and attitudes towards other characters. Selecting the right set of weaknesses is vital to setting up the plot and character arc.

Think your hero is too strong to have a weakness? Then he won't be very interesting to read about. He'd have to be the most amazing guy in the world for readers to slog through a whole book of his adventures. Even Superman and Batman have some issues, and exploring those is what makes reading about them interesting:

How does the hero overcome his problems?

Two Kinds of Weaknesses

1. Psychological weakness. This is some issue or behavior that might not seem like a problem, but over the course of the story is exposed as a problem.

In my novel Crush (which I've used as an example in other posts) the main character Simon doesn't go for relationships. He prefers casual hookups. He wants to be rich and he focuses most of his energy on work so he can succeed and eventually get rich. He's perfectly happy with his life and his goals.

Enter plot... in the form of a love interest. Once he meets Austin (it's a gay romance...) Simon realizes what he thought were fine values and behaviors mean might not be as he discovers he wants something else out of life. He realizes to succeed in his job he has to learn to cheat people. He has to rethink his personal goals and values.

The psychological weakness is something that hurts the hero. Selfishness, fear of something, attitude toward something. It doesn't feel like a weakness to him until the plot action makes him realize it.

2. Moral weakness. This takes things to a new level. A moral weakness is something that hurts others, and in a romance, a weakness that hurts the love interest.

Take Simon again. He doesn't want relationships. That's a psychological weakness until it affects Austin. Now it's a moral weakness. Simon's stance on relationships hurts

Austin, who would like to have a relationship with Simon. Until Simon can resolve his attitude about relationships, spending time with Austin does both more harm than good.

How do you find a moral weakness for your hero? It might be organic to the story you want to tell, and the change you want to create for your character. How will he become a better person in how he treats others (specifically the love interest if you're writing romance)? The starting point will be your moral weakness.

Look at the psychological weaknesses and find an immoral action that stems from them. What moral weakness does that imply for the character?

Another way is to take one of the hero's strengths and warp it into a weakness. A firefighter who is brave sounds like a hero. But if it leads him to take risks that put his crew in danger, it is a moral weakness. A cop or lawyer who blurs the edges of the law to get the bad guys are two more examples.

What strengths most define your hero? How can you exaggerate one into a negative? (Here's a list of strengths to work with.)

Take one of his virtues, and create a weakness that is completely the opposite. A hero who is scrupulously honest is hiding a terrible secret and it's hurting someone else until he owns up to the truth.

Once you have your character's weaknesses defined (the starting point), write down what corresponding value he will hold at the end of the story. How will each weakness be overcome or resolved to get him from the set of starting issues to the final values? That will give you plenty of ideas for the heart of the story.

A. Simon wants to be rich.—> B. Simon realizes there

are more important things than money.

How does Simon go from A to B? He realizes that to succeed in his job (and obtain wealth) he has to do things which hurt other people and might even be illegal. At first he brushes off the impact that has on him, but when Austin's family winery becomes the target, Simon finally realizes how much damage he is doing. He reevaluates both his goals and his behavior.

Two Main Characters

When you're writing romance, you will have two key characters. Should you do this process for both?

That depends, mainly on the length of the piece. In a novel, you can explore both characters' weaknesses, but in anything shorter, focus on the arc of just one character. Even in a novel, if you focus more on one character's journey you can do a better job of completing it satisfyingly, without rushing, skimping or dragging out the story too far past one character's resolution. If both characters clash and resolve their weaknesses in the same plot arc, then it might work. You don't need to give both main characters an equal number of scenes or treatment, even in a romance. Sometimes there's more drama and conflict when readers see (and identify with) more of one character's story.

Just be sure to choose the character who has the bigger weaknesses and travels the farthest in the story, the one who has lower lows. Readers will be drawn in by his dilemmas and the painful choices he has to make.

Your turn.

Go back to your Story Planning Worksheets and fine tune your character's beginning and ending points. If you've already written some of your dream scenes, take another look at them. Do they support the new character arc?

What kind of dream scenes do you now want to write?

Put them into the Dream Scene section of the Worksheet.

List of Character Traits

This list can help you create well-rounded characters not only by listing strengths your characters might exhibit, but by presenting an even more useful option for choosing character weaknesses.

1. Take the opposite of any strength to describe a weakness your character has and will overcome by the end of the story.

2. Exaggerate any of these strength until it becomes an obsession and you've created a new weakness.

Strengths of Wisdom and Knowledge: Cognitive strengths that entail the acquisition and use of knowledge

1. *Creativity [originality, ingenuity]*: Thinking of novel and productive ways to conceptualize and do things.

2. *Curiosity [interest, novelty-seeking, openness to experience]*: Taking an interest in ongoing experience for its own sake; exploring and discovering.

3. *Open-mindedness [judgment, critical thinking]*: Thinking things through and examining them from all sides; weighing all evidence fairly.

4. *Love of learning*: Mastering new skills, topics, and bodies of knowledge, whether on one's own or formally.

5. *Perspective [wisdom]*: Being able to provide wise counsel to others; having ways of looking at the world that make sense to oneself and to other people.

Strengths of Courage: Emotional strengths that involve the exercise of will to accomplish goals in the face of opposition, external and internal

6. *Bravery [valor]*: Not shrinking from threat, challenge, difficulty, or pain; acting on convictions even if unpopular.

7. *Persistence [perseverance, industriousness]*: Finishing what one starts; persisting in a course of action in spite of obstacles.

8. *Integrity [authenticity, honesty]*: Presenting oneself in a genuine way; taking responsibility for one's feeling and actions.

9. *Vitality [zest, enthusiasm, vigor, energy]*: Approaching life with excitement and energy; feeling alive and activated.

Strengths of Humanity: interpersonal strengths that involve tending and befriending others

10. *Love*: Valuing close relations with others, in particular those in which sharing and caring are reciprocated.

11. Kindness [generosity, nurturance, care, compassion, altruistic love, "niceness"]: Doing favors and good deeds for others.

12. *Social intelligence [emotional intelligence, personal intelligence]*: Being aware of the motives and feelings of other people and oneself.

Strengths of Justice: civic strengths that underlie healthy community life

13. *Citizenship [social responsibility, loyalty, teamwork]*: Working well as a member of a group or team; being loyal to the group.

14. *Fairness*: Treating all people the same according to notions of fairness and justice; not letting personal feelings bias decisions about others.

15. *Leadership*: Encouraging a group of which one is a member to get things done and at the same maintain time good relations within the group.

Strengths of Temperance: strengths that protect against excess

16. *Forgiveness and mercy*: Forgiving those who have done wrong; accepting the shortcomings of others; giving people a second chance; not being vengeful.

17. *Humility / Modesty*: Letting one's accomplishments speak for themselves; not regarding oneself as more special than one is.

18. *Prudence*: Being careful about one's choices; not taking undue risks; not saying or doing things that might later be regretted.

19. *Self-regulation [self-control]*: Regulating what one feels and does; being disciplined; controlling one's appetites and emotions.

Strengths of Transcendence: strengths that forge connections to the larger universe and provide meaning

20. *Appreciation of beauty and excellence [awe, wonder, elevation]*: Appreciating beauty, excellence, and/or skilled performance in various domains of life.

21. *Gratitude*: Being aware of and thankful of the good things that happen; taking time to express thanks.

22. *Hope [optimism, future-mindedness, future*

orientation]: Expecting the best in the future and working to achieve it.

23. *Humor [playfulness]*: Liking to laugh and tease; bringing smiles to other people; seeing the light side.

24. *Spirituality [religiousness, faith, purpose]*: Having coherent beliefs about the higher purpose, the meaning of life, and the meaning of the universe.

Understanding and Developing the Character Arc

You've probably heard of the character arc. If you've taken any writing classes, there is bound to be some discussion of it. If you're a new writer, take notes because you'll find this extremely valuable.

What's the main reason you keep reading a book?

It's not to find out what happens next, it's to find out what happens to the main characters. If it's well-written, then you will get sucked into their world and situation and care about them. You want the main character to win his challenge and achieve his goal.

You want him to jump through hoops or it's going to be boring, but we'll get to that later.

To engage readers with your characters, you need to show his challenge, his strengths and his weaknesses. And in most genres, the character will undergo some transformation as a result of the events, and the change is going to turn his world upside down, but it's the only way he can get his prize.

The sequence of internal changes are the character's arc. The events of the story (the plot) effect reactions and changes in the characters.

Let's look at an example. In the film *The Verdict,* Paul Newman's character is a washed-up alcoholic lawyer who has taken the easy way out and no longer has respect from anyone—including himself.

He takes on a medical malpractice suit because it looks like easy money. Along the way, he decides that if he takes the settlement, the doctor responsible for the injuries to the patient will get away with malpractice.

He has to fight some powerful political forces and even his client to bring the case to trial, and by the end he has regained his professional integrity and self-respect.

Not all characters have internal changes. Some have a realization, and others aren't supposed to change.

James Bond doesn't change. He comes in, kicks ass and gets the job done, whatever it takes. He kills people and loses colleagues and friends, but he keeps going. He can't afford to form attachments or he couldn't do his job.

Sometimes the change isn't for the better. In *The Godfather*, the youngest son is weak, not part of the family and trying to stay legitimate. After his father is killed, he takes revenge and ends up the new Godfather. He's strong, but he's gone to the dark side.

The kind of arc your character will have is entirely dependent on the genre of your book. I'll touch on that in Chapter 5. For now, let's talk about how to create characters and arcs that are compelling and make the plotting a lot easier.

There's another important aspect to mention about character arcs. Let's take a look at The Verdict again. The character starts off wanting easy money and not caring much about how he gets it. By the end he wants justice. He's changed his goal, right?

Not exactly. He wanted to get money, and he does, but when he changed what he expected about himself, his surface goal changed. This concept of surface and hidden goals will be important when we get to the worksheets on character building.

Build a Character Web

Leverage your supporting characters

All writers know that you need conflict and tension to drive to story forward, and to engage readers so they want to keep reading. In a thriller, writers can rely more on plot because the reader is there to see what happens next.

In romance the reader wants to know what happens to the characters and how will it affect their relationship. It's important to keep the level of conflict high, but readers will tune out if all you do is throw a new bump in the road to love.

Build a character web, and you won't have to always rely on the conflict between the main characters.

What's a character web?

It's a method of assigning roles to each main and supporting character that crosses alliances and conflicts between each character, and not just in relation to the main characters.

I'll use last year's NaNo novel as an example again. Austin is the Napa winemaker and Simon is the financial guy. There is a conflict between Austin and Simon over their backgrounds and goals, as well as an eventual conflict when Austin thinks Simon cozied up to him just to buy out his winery at a bargain price.

Now let's add in the supporting characters:

Simon's boss: He starts in an alliance with Simon. Then when he wants the winery (conflict with Austin), he pushes Simon to do things which harm the relationship with Austin (conflict with Simon and Austin). It also increases the underlying tension between Simon and Austin.

Austin's dad: He never really supported Austin (conflict with Austin). Later he and Simon end up in conflict. Eventually he'll end up in an alliance with Simon which helps Austin, and this will allow Austin and Simon to reconcile their differences.

Austin's brother: He appears to be in alliance with Austin, until we learn he's the cause of the financial problems which put the winery in jeopardy (conflict with Austin) and he resists Simon's suggestions for changes (conflict with Simon.)

Austin's assistant, Penny: She's on Austin's side (alliance with Austin). She's skeptical of Simon's suggestions (conflict with Simon), but eventually comes around (alliance with Simon). Then Austin's concern over Simon's true motives puts her back into conflict with Simon.

As you can see, conflicts and alliances between characters are fluid. You want this to happen as the story progresses. An original ally may become an enemy (Simon's boss) and an original enemy may become an ally (Austin's dad).

Not every subplot conflict has to get resolved, but the obstacles to the main couple getting together should be resolved in a way that eventually allows them to get together by the end of the story. Simon and his boss do not resolve their conflict, but other events occur so that conflict doesn't keep Simon and Austin apart.

If that sounds a bit complicated, just make a list of all your characters. Then write one or two sentences about their relationship with each of the other key characters, indicating whether it's an alliance or conflict and what the main element of that relationship entails.

Austin

Austin's assistant Penny is an alliance since she supports him in every way around the winery

Austin's brother Logan is an alliance since they run the winery together. Logan will become a conflict when the financial problems pile up.

Simon's boss is always in conflict with Austin.

Penny

In alliance with Austin

In conflict at first with Simon over meddling in winery finances

Begins alliance with Simon when she realizes his ideas are good

Begins a new conflict with Simon when she thinks he's trying to cheat Austin out of the winery.

If you're a spatial person as opposed to a list maker, write each character's name on a piece of paper, one in each corner. Then draw lines between each. Solid lines for alliances and dotted lines for conflicts, with a note about each connection. Once you start playing around with all the ways the characters connect, you'll see many other possibilities. (the image above isn't a good representation since the arrows don't go both ways, but in your story and your diagram, each character should have an effect on every other character, or at least on the main characters).

Conflict between Simon's boss and Austin's father

Conflict between Penny and Austin's brother

Depending on how long the story is, you may be able to explore these secondary conflicts in more detail. That's called subplot: when the conflict does not involve one of the main characters. In a novella, don't even think about it. You won't be able to resolve it without leaving loose threads of the main characters' conflict. In a novel, subplots can serve as a break so you're not always concentrating on the main characters and their issues.

In a romance, you want to show some good times between the main characters, but unless some conflict occurs, the story can quickly become boring. But such subplots can help keep some tension up while the main characters are enjoying a romantic moment. Even better: have the subplot intrude on the fun for the main characters. Always connect everything back to the main characters and their conflicts, or you can take too much of the spotlight from the main action of the story.

If you find that your stories get bogged down in the middle, reworking some of the conflicts with the supporting characters can help bring more excitement and tension in.

Chapter 4: Constructing the Story Skeleton

Download the Story Skeleton Worksheets from my website at **http://www.emlynley.com/Nano**

This chapter has another key set of exercises on the Story Skeleton Worksheet. Please download and print the PDFs.

Dream Scenes

By now you have a strong premise, several characters with layers, a set of steps your hero takes to reach his goal and a host of challenges his opponents will throw at him.

We're going to move to the Story Skeleton Worksheet.

I know Halloween is over, but bear with me. Remember, I said we weren't going to outline, and I want to keep my promise to you.

We're just going to come up with some ideas for scenes we'd like to write. These won't necessarily end up in the story, but a lot of them will.

Holly Lisle calls these "candy bar scenes" because they're fun to write. They are the kind of scenes that pop into your head when you're thinking about your story. I call them Dream Scenes.

At the top of the Story Skeleton Worksheet, write down your premise.

Now write down ten scenes that you would love to write for this book. Anything. Maybe you know what you want the first scene to be. Or the last scene. Or you can picture when the hero and the villain meet for the first time.

Write each scene idea down in a full sentence.

Tom sees Rita skinny dipping and decides to steal her from Joe.

Joe meets Tom and they instantly hate each other so much, they end up in a fistfight

List *at least ten* of these. Any order, no rhyme or reason. If you have more than ten, continue on the back of the paper, or just type them into your usual writing program or Scrivener outline.

Do make sure to include scenes with conflict, tension and disasters which happen to your hero as he pursues his goal.

Now go back to Step 7 on the Story Planning Worksheet (Reaching for the Desire), and see which of those ideas fit your new premise. You may need to tweak them a little.

Add them to the list of Dream Scenes.

Do any of them overlap or repeat? If so, then you know you'll want to use those scenes, because they fire up your imagination and excitement about your story and characters.

If you are one of those people who like index cards, go grab a bunch and write one Dream Scene summary on each one. Now lay them out on the floor, your bed, or the pool table, and start shuffling them around until you get an idea for a sequence.

If you're using Scrivener, you can write a "card" for each scene and shuffle them around visually in the program.

If you don't like index cards, you can write the list in Word or in a spreadsheet and just rearrange them manually.

If you've got the conflict scenes, try to order them so the problems and aftermath of each one makes your hero progressively more distressed. You want to show his arc and if he has a run-in with his opponent and they get in a fistfight, the next confrontation can't be the opponent kicking sand in his fact. They've already escalated their dislike past.

Rearrange all the other Dream Scene cards around those in ways that make sense. What leads up to a conflict scene? What happens after a big scene?

Keep juggling these sequences around.

If you're doing this on a spreadsheet or Word doc, you may want to save different versions so you can go back and compare two different potential sequences.

If you use Scrivener, you can save a snapshot of each different possibility. It's also very easy to move scenes around later, even after you've written them.

Write down five possible scene ideas for your opening scene.

Write five possibilities for your final scene.

Then put all the scene ideas and cards away. It's not time to write yet. I'd like to show you a few more useful techniques first. While you're not planning your story, your brain is going to be synthesizing all the elements we've just been working on. I can almost guarantee that as soon as you close the program or put your Worksheets into your project folder, you'll get an idea you want to add.

That's great. Just write it down in the appropriate section, or start a new page in your idea notebook. You will be taking a look at those before you start writing, and during the writing process as well.

Another Word on Plot

Because this process is all about planning your novel, and getting your foundation built, I haven't spent a lot of time sewing up the plot. We've touched on some ideas for scenes, and put them in a rough order, and we have a good idea where the turning point scenes will be, and how they will end up, even if we don't know exactly what happens during any of these scenes.

A scene summary like "Doug goes to the bank to plan the robbery" is clear, but it's incredibly vague, so you still have complete control over what he does, what he says, who he speaks to, what he notices, every single action and detail is still up for grabs.

If you're a pantser, that's all you need.

If you've been a plotter, you may be breaking out in a sweat because you don't know exactly what's going to happen or how it's going to tie into the next scene and the one after that, and the thirty scenes that come later.

Relax. It's not necessary. Please trust me on this one.

I used to be a die-hard plotter. All my planning and prep centered around what would happen when, and I struggled with sequence and how to get from A to B to C. I stressed over details that stopped my writing process.

And when I did get the books finished and published I got a lot of the same comments in my reviews: interesting plot, but the characters didn't really do that much for me.

Characters were my big weakness. I didn't spend much time on them. I didn't really know how to build an interesting character. So I spent a lot of time on finding out how. I probably have fifteen books on characterization, character development, traits, etc.

But it wasn't until I peeled back even more layers the desire/need/weaknesses that I finally discovered why those elements were so vital to decide on before anything else.

The first book where everything clicked just flowed from my brain to my fingertips. I was soaring too, because it had never happened for me. Writing was always work.

I realized I had been doing the heavy lifting for the characters, pushing them here and there and literally making them jump through hoops. It was exhausting.

But when I started with character, the beauty of the process revealed itself.

I didn't need to decide what the characters would, they would tell me, because that's what that character would do in that specific situation.

Each character views a situation from his unique perspective and reacts as only he can.

Let's take a plot point like the character getting into car accident on the way to his son's high school graduation.

If my character is a very laid-back person who isn't too stuck on rules, and knows everything works out in the end, he'll just exchange numbers and keep going.

If he's a little compulsive, he might take forty photos with his phone and take photos of the other driver, their driver's license and get names and address for every witness.

If the character is in the middle of a divorce he might find the accident as a perfect excuse to get out of going to the damn graduation in the first place.

I didn't make that stuff up, the characters did it on

their own. All I did was decide who they are, and then what happens comes naturally.

It was the most exciting revelation I had since I started writing.

But once I figured it out, I could let go of the security blanket of an elaborate plot, and I could have a lot of fun with these characters.

And I started getting better reviews too. I don't doubt for a millisecond that there is a connection. The planning experience now is one I find very enjoyable and I'm always excited about starting a new project. I don't find myself intimidated at the thought of having at least 50,000 words between the first one and THE END.

I know I'm going to enjoy the process, and all the surprises in store, but never worry that I have to know exactly what's supposed to happen next. It's going to happen without my intervention.

Start with a Bang

I know I promised we wouldn't outline anything, and I'm not going to break my promise to you. But there are a few specific scenes I suggest you think very carefully about before you write a word. If that means outlining, or making a list of ideas, then do what works for you.

The Opening Scene

We have five different ideas for the opening scene from the Story Skeleton Worksheet.

Now in the Opening Scene section, write down your character's main traits, his strengths and weaknesses.

In addition to reading dozens of writing books and taking another dozen or so classes, I've studied screenwriting techniques too. When it comes to showing character and conflict, screenwriters are masters at concentrating the important elements to their essence.

Using their methods, you can really nail your opening scene. And once you've got that going, you'll be on a high and will be able to keep writing.

The screenwriting secret to opening scene is to introduce your hero. These are the key elements:

- Challenge the lead character—this will get the reader to care about him and show us a preview of the bigger challenges he'll deal with in the book.
- Show us his special skill—make sure each character

has something he is proficient at.

- Have him overcome the challenge by using the special skill—we love winners, and if we see him mastering this problem, we'll be on his side from page one.
- Lead the character and reader into the next chapter by ending on a new and bigger problem.

If your character yells at his bratty sister in the first scene, he's not going to endear himself to the reader, no matter how justified his behavior is.

If he is a dog lover, and the first scene shows his dog getting off the leash and he spends all night looking for the dog, then sits outside the pound and charms the first person who shows up for work to let him in, then the reader is going to care a lot about him.

If you choose to have your opening scene be the kickoff to the bigger challenge, he might not be able to win right away. So, break the problems down into smaller elements, so he can at least win one, no matter how small.

It takes some thought to do this well. You'll want to look at his strengths and figure out an appropriate problem that will demonstrate his expertise and a key element of his personality.

Then, just as you've lulled the reader into liking your character, cheering him on and enjoying his little victory, sock them with a bigger problem that's a lead-in to the main conflict of the book.

They won't be able to turn the page fast enough.

If you're already writing, do your best to get the four

key elements in the first chapter. You can work on heightening each element later when you do a revision.

Where Are We?

One element that wasn't part of the Story Planning Worksheet is the setting of your book. I haven't forgotten it, just pulling it out to a later step in the process so you can focus on the biggest elements of the story, which are the characters.

Setting is incredibly important. Some people know immediately where to set their story—in fact some stories can only happen in a particular place, such as fantasy or sci-fi story where world building is vital.

Some stories can happen anywhere. Other stories don't suggest a particular setting until you have more of the foundation planned. Now you know who your main characters are and the kind of problems they face, and you can select a setting that best portrays the story you've begun to construct.

Screenwriting can teach us a lot about setting. Unless it's a big-budget film, the production won't take place in too many different locations, so the writer and director need to be creative with how they use setting.

You can have different sections of your story in different settings to portray the type of conflict the hero faces. For example, if your hero is a college student who is facing a choice about what to study—what he loves, say painting, or a subject for which he has a full-ride scholarship, engineering—and his family is pressuring him, then certain conflicts and events will naturally happen in a setting associated with the family, and other scenes will naturally be set in a place representing his joy of painting.

Choose some settings that represent particular challenges or emotions of the main characters.

Setting can have a very big influence on character. Here are some more ways to think about the interplay of setting and other elements of the story.

Setting Impacts Character

We've talked a lot about developing layers for your characters, building the character arc and using supporting characters to increase the conflict in a story. Now I want to demonstrate how to use setting to bring in yet another layer to your characters.

Setting encompasses time period, geographic location and even social status, but most of the time it describes physical locations. All people have places that mean something to them, good or bad. You may remember where you made your first home run, had your first kiss, or the swing set where you fell and lost a tooth. Going to those places evokes memories and emotions.

You probably also have places you feel comfortable and safe: your home, a favorite park, a coffee shop you frequent. You may also have places you consider your territory: your office, your den, your car.

Now let's give each of your characters places where he feels safe/happy/comfortable and some reasons why. These may or may not also be his territory, and if someone else approaches he may feel threatened or protective.

In my book *An Intoxicating Crush*, which I've been using as an example for many of my techniques, Simon the finance guy feels at home in his office. He loves his work and focuses most of his energy there. When we move Simon out of his office he gets uncomfortable.

Austin, the winemaker, loves spending time in the vineyards—outside in the sunshine—where he can connect with the vines, the soil, the grapes. He brings Simon here, but Simon's not comfortable in Austin's world at first, then gradually as his feelings for Austin change, so does his enjoyment of being outside.

Let's take another example: Austin is wealthy and has a large house full of antiques. Simon watches his money, so his apartment is small with furniture just a notch above Ikea. When Simon is at Austin's he's overwhelmed by the luxurious surroundings and feels out of place. This will spill over into his interactions with Austin, not just when they are at Austin's house.

Simon's house is comfortable for him, but when Austin visits, Simon feels self-conscious that he doesn't have nice things. He's not threatened by Austin's presence, but by his perceptions of Austin's attitudes—even when they are wrong. Setting a scene in Simon's house automatically sets up tension and conflict between these two characters, even when the scene does not contain conflict in dialog or action. Simon is off-guard and defensive, and Austin doesn't understand why. It sets the scene up for some great dynamics no matter whose POV we choose.

Let's sum up ways to build characters through setting;

1. Give each character a zone where he feels comfortable. You may want to introduce that character in his comfort zone, if you want to paint a strong personality picture for the reader. In *Crush*, Austin's first appearance has him running from his own office and financial issues and out into the vineyard where he feels safe to think about what's going wrong with his business. Provide reasons for why the character feels comfortable in this place. Write them down in your character notes and circle the location so you can set specific scenes here late.

2. Give the character zones of discomfort and reasons why. Remember these and use these settings for scenes you

want added conflict or tension for the character. Sometimes these can be much more interesting and provide added insight to character and back-story, without info-dumping. Show a character's discomfort in these settings, and you'll eliminate a lot of telling and explaining. Spend some time constructing these zones and reasons for the character's behavior.

If you write suspense or thrillers, you'll want a lot of these uncomfortable zones and plenty of reasons why they make the MC uncomfortable. Think about *Vertigo*: the main character, Scottie, is afraid of heights. Hitchcock shows us this with an opening scene where someone dies as a result of his fear. High places are a setting where the character is uncomfortable. One key scene in the film is when he's again in this zone of discomfort, which sets up the tension before anything even happens.

Send the character into these zones to up the suspense and danger, both internal and external, depending on the type of stories you write. Readers love to see characters pushed into danger zones and will keep reading to see how they handle the situation.

Like the section about character weakness, you can spot the trend: give your characters problems and pile on some more. If your character can overcome his fear/hatred/etc., of the danger zones, then it becomes part of the character arc. What event forces him to do that? See how the setting plus solid characterization almost writes the plot for you?

3. Explore how each character acts when someone enters his comfort zone. Does he welcome the others? Does he feel territorial? Use these responses again for increased tension and conflict. His response will differ for each other

character. Which supporting characters are part of his "team" when he needs to protect his zone, and which represent an additional source of conflict?

4. How does each character act with respect to other characters' comfort zones? Is he aggressive, knowing he's not welcome, but entering anyway? Is he timid and waits for an invitation? Does he fail to act out of respect for someone else's zone, with negative consequences?

5. Force your characters out of their comfort zones and force others to enter someone else's zone to increase the drama.

6. Keep some places neutral. Setting scenes in neutral places means neither is at an emotional disadvantage.

7. Have a setting which is a comfort zone for one character, but a danger zone for another. A person who was bullied in school will have a different reaction to a visit to his old high school than the quarterback jock for whom the school represents wonderful memories.

A beach sounds idyllic, but what if one character's little sister drowned on a Hawaiian vacation? It won't make a nice vacation spot for these two when one has a negative reaction to a place that's generally a comfortable or pleasant zone.

Turn to your Story Skeleton Worksheet and let's drill down to some more specifics than we did in the Story Planning Worksheet.

Character Introductions

In "Start with a Bang," I mentioned the screenwriting technique of an opening scene that draws the reader into the character's world with an immediate challenge he can overcome.

It's called character introduction and you can use this technique with your other key characters in order to create vivid and lasting first impressions of each one.

Screenwriters use this technique as a way to entice big actors to want a role in their script. The key is to make the first scene with a character so unforgettable that the actor can't wait to jump into his skin. Actors love playing characters with layers and challenges. No one wants to play a boring guy who has boring lines. An actor will leap at the chance to play a scene-stealing character, even if the character doesn't have a lot of screen time. As long as the role is memorable, the actor will be remembered.

The way to set that up is to make the character's entrance memorable, but it also has to show the essence of that character in a way that the reader will remember.

For your second main character and your villain, take a look at the traits you created on the Story Planning Worksheet.

Which trait is most representative of the character? What aspect of his personality do you want to highlight? Build a scene around that, and design the very first glimpse of the character—or his first line of dialog to hit the reader in the face with big personality.

If you're character loves to climb mountains, you

could show the first glimpse of him just reaching the summit (overcoming a challenge). How does he react? Make the first thing he says or does something only he would say or do.

Your mountain-climbing fellow is also a coffee addict. The first thing he does is pull out a few sticks, light a fire and boil some water to make coffee. (Assuming he's not in an area where this is prohibited).

Or he sings a song at the top of his lungs because he's really into music.

You know what makes your character tick, so show the reader immediately.

On the Story Skeleton Worksheet, write down what the first indelible image of your character should be.

Now do the same thing for the villain. Do you want to show him doing something bad? Or do you want to show him in a good light, and then surprise the reader when he's not the good guy?

Let's take an example of a villain who loves Chinese calligraphy. He studies it and our first glimpse is him putting the finishing touches on a particularly challenging character and he's thrilled and proud of his efforts to finally master it. He might hold it up and enjoy the beauty of the character. So far, we probably like this guy. He's got a cool skill and he's demonstrated some expertise.

Then an assistant comes into the room and gives him some bad news, and our calligrapher responds by throwing the ink well at the messenger and ruining his suit, then demanding the assistant clean up the mess.

Now we see who he really is. Which image stays with the reader? The brutality of his reaction to the assistant, certainly. But we won't forget that beautiful Chinese character, and the paradox you've demonstrated will keep readers intrigued by the character: what is he hiding? Are other characters hiding something? You've given the villain a mix of good and bad traits, and that's entertaining too.

Once you catch the reader off guard, you have got them hooked, and you've proved you aren't going to take the obvious path in your story. They'll keep reading, eager for the next surprise you have in store.

Jot down some ideas of how to introduce your villain into the story on the Skeleton sheet.

Remember you can combine this with other techniques such as a demonstration of safe zones, danger zones, or hinting at the bigger conflict to come. If you're working on your first book, just aim to get the basics. You can try the more advanced techniques once you get the hang of the most essential elements. Or try weaving those in when you're revising the story, after November 30.

Introducing supporting characters

You won't want to employ this technique for every character. Save it for the most important characters. Try to keep the others from stealing the scenes or becoming too memorable, unless you intend for that to happen. It's a powerful technique to introduce a character who may get a spin-off story in another book.

Generally, when a character enters with a bang, the reader is going to expect him to be a big part of the story. If a very likable character doesn't have a big part, you run the risk of disappointing some readers who like him more than your more important characters.

Snapshots

Now is the time I start fleshing out my character in the way most people start. I choose hair color, eyes, height, body type. Some of these will suggest themselves, based on who the character is inside or his job, or the setting of the story.

Sometimes I used the character development worksheets with birthdays, siblings names, father's profession, etc., and other times I wait until I'm writing and I need to know. It might slow me down a little, but I like the flexibility to create the details I need as I'm writing.

However, if you get value out of those worksheets, or feel more comfortable with the information written down in one place, that's great.

If you have a picture in your mind of a character, then draw it, or find photos online who embodies your character.

One thing I love to do is house hunting for my characters. I know what city they live in and what kind of house they would have, so I can go to the real estate listings in that city and find an appropriate house in a neighborhood that fits the story. I'll save images into a folder on my computer. I tend to use my creativity on my story and I don't have as much left over for interior decorating and architecture, so the 360 degree views available on so many real estate websites are a wonderful resource for me.

I'll also save images of the kind of clothes they would wear, menus from restaurants they would eat at and I bookmark restaurant reviews and check Google maps for their town, if I've never visited it.

Chapter 5: Background Research and Reading

The Least You Need

Depending on the world where I've set my story, I tend to use between 10 and 30 reference books for a novel. I like to immerse myself in the world of the characters, so I know a winemaker would see a situation or react to the weather, for example.

If you've got time for that, fantastic. If not, grab a couple of books from the library and skim them before you start writing. You can always go back later and fill in specifics if you get stuck during the actual writing.

I do suggest keeping a Word doc, or a notes clipboard in Scrivener for questions you come up with as you write. Anything that stops the story should probably get looked up right away, but you can smooth over everything else until later.

No matter how much research I do, I still have lots of gaps in my knowledge. I save that for revision, and I'll show you how to do that in the next section.

Do get an idea for geography of the place you are writing about. Bookmark the local newspaper website so you can pull a relevant fact or event into your story.

If you are writing a historical novel, or one based in science fact, then you'll have to do extra homework before you start writing. It may require fairly extensive research, so plan ahead the best you can if you intend to write one of these more challenging genres for your NaNo. I admit to playing it fairly safe for November, and choosing a contemporary setting I can easily research online, so I'm not scrambling to fill in too many blanks.

If you find out something you hung the plot on isn't invented until 30 years later, then you can just call it steampunk or fantasy, and no one will mind. But if there is something that vital to your story, it should be the first thing you research before you even start plotting.

I always start out with a notebook for each novel, with pertinent information, but before I even start writing I tend to abandon the thing, or I forget to look in at for all the gems of information I scribbled inside. So far, I've managed to do fine without it, so maybe my brain retained some of the information anyway.

Choose whatever method works for you, or experiment with a good information organization system. If you like to keep notes online, or in your phone, don't mess with success.

Just keep track of the most important information, and keep another list of missing information to research later.

With those two sheets, and the planning you've done, you will be ready to start laying down words.

The Beauty of Brackets

Brackets [ ] are my secret weapon during a first draft.

With brackets, you never have to stop typing until you want to. I use brackets for anything and everything I don't know while I'm writing, things I haven't decided yet, or even words I can't remember. I'll even use them for scenes.

I had one manuscript with [lastname] in there about forty times. There was even a character whose first name I hadn't decided on and used [friend] when I needed to.

Can't put your finger on the word you want, then do this [like "confused" but not that word].

Don't know whether your character is going north or south: He moved [direction] toward the [thing he's trying to get to].

I like using brackets better than comment bubbles, because I can actually count all the [in the manuscript and know exactly how much work I have ahead of me.

I'm not the only one of my group of erotic romance authors to use [sex scene here]. In fact, I have a friend who didn't use my method to search for all the brackets in her story, and sent one with [sex scene here] to her publisher. When she got the manuscript back for edits, the editor had left a comment "Now would be a good time for that." With a smiley face.

So give yourself permission to [ ] anything you can't quickly remember or find out so you don't interrupt your flow of writing.. No one is going to see them but you. Plus, the words in the brackets get counted for NaNo, while a comment bubble doesn't. Not that we're splitting hairs, but it never hurts.

Then, after you type THE END, you will have plenty of time to go and fill in the brackets, making decisions, consulting the thesaurus, or researching the gaps in knowledge.

Filling in the Gaps

Keep in mind during November that you're just writing a first draft. You would be highly unlikely to finish something ready to publish, so don't worry if it's not perfect.

You will have gaps, missing information, maybe even missing scenes because you just weren't sure what should happen *right there,* and stopping to figure it out would take too much time.

Even published authors keep plowing ahead when something doesn't spring to mind, and get on with the rest of the story, knowing it will get sorted out on the next draft.

In the event you get to THE END without any gaps, missing scenes, brackets or any of the usual hazards, chances are that you'll still find something to fix or change when you read it again. And you should.

No matter how certain I am while writing page 1 that I have all the elements in place, I always end up with a slightly different story than I expect. That entails reworking some of the early chapters to set the book back on track toward the new destination, or push the characters along a slightly different path, because I found one better than my original plan.

I won't attempt to give you any advice for revising your manuscript here, but you will absolutely have an opportunity to fill in the gaps and correct the inevitable errors and inconsistencies. So don't let the gaps hold you back. Leap right over them to land on solid ground, and keep running!

Chapter 6: Ready, Set, NaNo!

Now the Fun Begins

You're now ready to write, armed with your premise, your characters' arcs, your list of key scenes and turning points, and a darn good idea of how this will all wrap up. You know how all the characters will interact and who will betray whom and you know what problems you're going to throw at your main characters.

All you need to do is stitch the tapestry together with words.

And this is the fun part.

All the planning and organizing should have gotten you excited about your story, ready to meet your characters and follow them down the road, with a few unplanned excursions here and there as they take you for the ride of your life.

Just keep typing fast enough and you'll be able to keep up with them.

By getting to know who your characters are inside, what they want, what they fear, what they love and what they will do to protect what's important, I hope you've discovered you want to spend the next intense month with these people.

If you find you don't like them, then you still have time to make some changes, shuffle some characteristics, and patch them up. Because if you don't love your heroes, you can't expect a reader will love them either.

By the Numbers

You already know the magic number 1667 words per day for the whole month of November.

It sounds a very daunting number, and for me it used to feel like an impossibility. I always dreaded the days when I didn't have any clue what to write. They outnumbered the days when I was too busy or tired to write.

One piece of advice: don't stop at your 1667 if you still have ideas and you're not falling asleep on your keyboard. Better to bank some extra words when you can, in case something unexpected keeps you from writing.

How long does it take to write 1667 words?

I can write on average 1000 words an hour when I'm not distracted and when I know what I want to write, so I'd say about two hours, tops.

If you split it into two one-hour sessions it will feel less overwhelming. I often say I'll sit down and get down at least 500 words and before I know it I'm at 750 or 1000.

If you can get 3 one-hour sessions in on the weekends, you can get a head start on the week.

I have a friend who texts herself a few sentences at a time when she's waiting for the bus or eating lunch, whenever she has two or three spare minutes. She collects them all when she gets home and keeps going wherever she left off.

You'll find the methods that work best for you. Try a few sessions during October to see how long it takes to write 500 words off the top of your head. You may be surprised how little time it takes when the ideas are flowing.

Unless you're already used to writing every day, you may find it very difficult to sit down and be productive, especially when the pressure's on.

It's one of the reasons we filled in the worksheets and planned a lot of the story in advance, and came up with a list of Dream Scenes. I've suggested how to write your first few scenes, and some of the key scenes later in the book, so you have a good head start with inspiration.

What to do when you really just don't know what should happen next? Ask your characters!

If you've just finished a scene in the hero's POV, ask one of the other characters what his reaction is to what just happened, or what he should do next.

By now you know what makes each character tick, who his allies and opponents are and what he's secretly searching for. He should have a response. If not, ask another character. Eventually one of them will have something to say, which will get you writing again.

You can always choose another Dream Scene from the list. Get started on something that's already fairly clear in your brain, and it will motivate you. No one says you have to write the story in order.

Once you've got the next Dream Scene finished, go back and fill in the blanks until your previous scene meets up with the Dream Scene.

Still feeling at a loss? Throw a new problem at your hero. Then double it. If he hates dogs, have him confronted with five of them. He'll have plenty to say about that. If it doesn't fit into the bigger picture, you can toss it later (after November 30). In the meantime it will give you deeper insight into your character's limits.

You can keep going back to your story skeleton worksheet and adding more ideas for Dream Scenes, or rearranging the order of scenes. Sometimes this will provide more ideas.

Stop by the Smooth Draft website during November for more ideas and writing prompts you can use in any story. (www.smoothdraft.com)

Chapter 7: Lather, Rinse, Repeat

Hopefully you found the worksheets and my process helpful for planning your novel. They can be used for any length of story, though you won't need as many threads to the storyline for a short story or a novella.

I use the process over and over, and find new ways to tweak it every time. The more you use it, the less time it will take you to go through the steps. I can put together a novel plan in a day or two, though I like to spend a little more time on it and get about 20-30 Dream Scenes before I start writing. That gets me most of the way through a novel, with just enough gaps to leave room for random ideas while I'm writing.

I'd love to know what you think of the process, and how it's worked for you. Let me know if it helped you finish a book during NaNo.

Even if it didn't help, I would like to hear from you to find out why. If the steps aren't clear, or you didn't have enough to start writing, please email me your feedback. I intend to do a revised version, taking into account reader's experiences in order to improve this guide.

Email me: em@smoothdraft.com

Or visit http://www.smoothdraft.com and use the Contact form.

I'd love to hear about any books you contract or

publish, using on the methods I've shared in this book.

Thank you, and happy writing!

About the Author

EM Lynley, bestselling author, Rainbow Award winner and EPPIE finalist, has worked in high finance, high tech, and in the wine industry. She spent 10 years as an economist and financial analyst, including a year as a White House Staff Economist, but only because all the intern positions were filled. Tired of boring herself and others with dry business reports and articles, her creative muse is back and naughtier than ever. She has lived and worked in London, Tokyo and Washington, D.C., but the San Francisco Bay Area is home for now.

She writes Gay Romance with Taste. Find her online:

Website: www.emlynley.com
Blog: http://blog.emlynley.com/
Facebook: www.facebookcom/emlynley
Twitter: http://twitter.com/emlyney
Smooth Draft Editing: http://www.smoothdraft.com

Lynley also owns Smooth Draft Editing and offers writing and revising tips in a twice-monthly newsletter. Visit http://www.smoothdraft.com for more information.

www.ingramcontent.com/pod-product-compliance
Lightning Source LLC
LaVergne TN
LVHW091009080826
845145LV00003B/1186

* 9 7 8 0 6 1 5 9 0 0 8 7 2 *